allowing for time

Erika Evans

the poems & art of an austin artist

Burlwood Books | Austin

BURLWOOD BOOKS

Austin, Texas
BurlwoodBooks.com

First published in the United States of America
by Burlwood Books 2023

Text copyright © 2023 estate of Erika Evans
Photos copyright © 2023 estate of Erika Evans

Cover painting by Erika Evans

Cover design by Olivia Hammerman
www.ochbookdesign.com

ISBN 979-8-9850784-6-6

1. Poetry 2. Relationships—Poetry 3. Art

This book is dedicated to all the artists out there, either just starting out or well down the road.

And to everyone who has ever been in an abusive relationship. There is help. There is always help. And you are not alone. Please reach out to a friend or family member. Or call the National Domestic Violence Hotline at (800) 799-7233. They will answer any time, any day.

You are not alone, and there is always help.

All proceeds from this book will benefit the victims of domestic violence, including donations to the following groups.

SAFE Austin

The Christi Center

"I feel like poetry **allows for time** to be given to something you want to say. Whenever you say something normally in conversation, I feel like it evaporates immediately and people hold on to that in their memory, and it becomes distorted. At least when you have it in a poem form, you can reflect back on it and have a more tangible thing to look at."

-Erika Evans

From the Editor

I first met Erika in 2022, when I saw her typing poems in front of Guero's, a restaurant on South Congress Avenue in Austin, Texas. I was part of a group of poets called Typewriter Rodeo, and we did the same thing—typed poems on the spot for strangers—all over Austin. Between poems, I chatted with Erika and was immediately struck by her energy and sincerity. She had a way with people, especially ones she'd never met.

Over the next few months, I stopped by Erika's spot, talking with her about the weird but satisfying art of writing poems for strangers. Eventually, I asked if she'd like to join a Typewriter Rodeo event. Her eyes lit up. No, not just her eyes. It was her whole presence. The sun is a huge part of Austin, and it may be an overworked metaphor, but still—Erika looked like part of the sun was shining from beneath that hat. She glowed. And said heck yes she wanted to join us!

The day before our event I messaged Erika, saying I was looking forward to typing with her. The day of, she didn't show. And I never heard from her.

Not long after, a friend who played violin on South Congress told me what had happened: Erika had been murdered while on a trip with an abusive male companion in Portland, Oregon. And her family was doing a small tribute that weekend, near her spot outside Guero's.

I went to the tribute, sat down with my typewriter, and wrote Erika a poem. I didn't know what else to do. That poem, and the message I wrote to Erika's family, are on the next two pages. I left the poem in the book of tributes, and eventually Erika's dad reached out to me. He gave me her typewriter (which continues to make poetry magic as part of our group), and I offered to do this book. I can only imagine how different things might have been, if Erika had been able to do that first event with us, and so many more.

Several of the poems in here include responses from the people Erika wrote them for. I hope this book honors her memory and soul, with even the slightest slant of sun she brought so many.

Sean Petrie, April 2023, Austin, TX

*'Oregon Live' article
about Erika*

From Erika's dad

Erika Evans

Poet, Artist, Musician, and Writer
Bachelor of Arts, The University of Texas at Austin, 2018

Born in Austin, Erika shared her love of literature and the arts with a delightful creative energy that seemed limitless. An avid traveler, she was always interested in a new adventure. In addition to her musical performances, song writing, travel blogs, and acrylic on canvas paintings, Erika wrote hundreds of poems during the last years of her precious life.

In dedication to her memory, this collection is a portfolio showcasing Erika's essence and exceptional understanding of the human existence. She downplayed her unique ability to express a concept or topic through poetry, yet her work serves as a lasting legacy for all to enjoy.

The proceeds of this book will assist many other victims of domestic violence.

May 10, 1996 - September 23, 2022

Austin Monthly
article

Orange Magazine
article

3

For Erika
(written by Sean Petrie, Oct. 1, 2022)

Can you hear it?
These keys?
Right here behind me, at Guero's
Here in your spot
There is some Hendrix playing
All along the watchtower
This spot where you watched
Where you typed
Where you touched
The hearts lives dreams
Of so many
I don't know what to type
For you
Except thank you
Except you
Were heard
You were seen
Even for too brief a time
I hope you can hear this
I hope you know
How much hope you gave.
Sometimes poetry
Doesn't have the answers
Sometimes all you can do
Is say thanks
For the time
The moment
The connection you did have
However brief,
(And just now, as I am typing this
A couple stopped, leaned down
Smiled and said thanks.
They had no idea what for.
I think you would have liked that.)

"To Erika's family: I'm sure you know this, but she brought a lot of joy and connection to so many people. So many strangers. She made people feel seen, understood. That is a gift. And her sharing that, even for way too brief of a time, is just so special. All those poems she wrote? Over all the years? So many of those are framed or tacked onto people's refrigerators, tucked into journals. She had such a huge, positive impact on so many lives."

Poems for Others

These poems were all written by Erika on the spot on her typewriter, when a stranger came up and gave her a topic. As much as possible, the original formatting is preserved.

Several poems also have a note from the recipient.

All paintings are by Erika.

Adventuring a new

wrangling them in
tearing it down
tearing it down
This town ain't too big
as we can clearly see
the end of it on the one side of this
bar, the other at its parking lots
edge
one of us will need to budge
a free wheeling
composite of griefs wisdom and
happinessess deposits

i'm ready to go for you're the one
who holds the grudge
and there's more to see
beyond this sage brush

"I was visiting Austin when I ran into Erika and immediately knew I needed a poem from her! I keep it in my room in a cute glass frame, such a fun memory from Texas!"

Birthday Blitz

The sky never falls around you
instead it hangs suspended
 like a perfect halo surrounding you
 adorned with stars

You stand so tall-
 I could not have missed you, despite
 all of 'entropy's' attempts
  at fandangoing lateness
  and tossing aside performances of
chivalry
and what's there to thank-
    just you
   acting like a beacon
    for some love-motivated
    search party

Let There Be Light

It is time now
to take this walk
    making steady paces across the
    heavy traffic-laden street

    I dodge eighteen wheelers with
      ease , the ambush of
    tractors and log hauling mega
trucks
  This is life's candid expression
      of itself
I've no need to be sad
    but I will indulge it
      regardless from time to time
        beating on the same old drum
    of those preceding me
living out the narrative
    remembering at times
      that I'd written it

Chapter of Determination

it seemed like for so long
we'd been spinning idly
toiling away
without true intention or motive
    now a certain
purposefulness has come about
  a raunchy sort of turn around
from simple sitting
to leisurely swaying
sauntering under a moon
that previously was empty
    Now it's as astonishing to live
every morning a miracle

*"Words cannot explain the immense gratitude we have for
her beautiful words and having blessed us with such beautiful
messages. She wrote this after I explained to her that I was
going through a lot of change in a short period of time, a break
up, moving to Austin, etc. and every morning for a couple of
weeks I would read her poem to myself to remind myself about
something so beautiful she saw in me, that I was having a hard
time seeing for myself. She was a beautiful and thoughtful
writer."*

From the perspective of a rose

it may only be able to tell
 in moments where the
  petals are in such an incredible flux
 that it is blooming
 in the height of an emotional overture
  the seed is planted
  readied for the water to come and rain
          upon its encasement
the roots come up
and then down deeply into the dirt
   inspiring the worms
   enlivened by words
        responsive and amenable

**It's beena
filthy good time**

   ridding myself of the
      staunch obsessive quality
   consumed
with a crutch
 I've lost it now
 walking away from the
      taste once in my mouth
it's so much more electric
    the world is
high-def
    the ladies
   reel and squeal
 the lights of night
   are brighter
just by virtue of this new
   walk of life

**Birthed into
a new realm**

This isn't a death
it's more so a passing on into
a new realm
Some speculate that we reincarnate
into every life
and then once that's done we can
finally go on and out from Earth
Perhaps the Dog
  (God spelled backwards)
has already mastered this rebirth

*"I remember the day I met Erika downtown. I was grieving
my dog's passing. Erika wrote this poem for me and her words
brought real tears to my eyes & comfort to my heart, i only
met her for a brief moment but I could tell she was a special
soul."*

a magical world

To know you is magical in itself
     to love you, even greater
     there is nothing like a bond between
     brother and sis
It is noticeable from even several meters away
    Radiating a special sort of light
     one almost otherworldly heavenly

Some may suggest it could be attributed to
   the length
of days spent together, the overall time,
or even the tendency for those sharing similar
    genes to get along so swimmingly
    but there is one thing we know for sure
to know you inspires so much love from my heart
    that together we reside
     in a magical world all our own.

For so long

for so long I've known you
and for so long we've grown
Almost as if we'd been planted here together
   Our roots went deep
   tying knots together beneath the
      mountains , reaching deep to the
   arterial core
     but now as our hands clasp
     we ignite interest of passerby
      for this sort of love
        is one that's rare to find

"I wasn't a friend of Erika's, just a stranger on the street, but she left a lasting impression and her poem is an incredible part of my life. We had some friends visiting from out of town and took them to Guero's for some Austin vibes. I was waiting on the curb outside to leave and Erika was sitting with her typewriter, in an old timey dress and I was immediately drawn to her: it's not a normal sight to see someone time-traveling on Congress! When I went to see what she was all about, she explained her pop-up poetry, based on only a few provided details. I asked her to write a poem for my upcoming wedding. I told her that my fiance and I had been friends since childhood, that nature held great sway in our lives, and that we were eloping in a field at the foot of our favorite mountain. She encapsulated in just a few stanzas the depth of our relationship and the hopeful, magical, beautiful version of our type of love. Even the typo feels right. We actually made the poem a key part of our wedding, a focal point.

I will never forget that night, the urge to speak to Erika, and the immediate yes to asking her for a poem. I hope in this terrible time, you feel some warmth knowing that she had such an impact, created beauty, and made people happy."

On the Come Up

why the life lived
feels at time like forgery

I'd woken up in these bones
    disjointed as it seems
disconnected were my head and my heart
    syncopation
One moment bliss, the next trembling
What is this? some sort of spiritual
    profundity-
      I feel half-baked and then I
      recall- What's at stake?
      and the rhythm returns
   I'm a veteran Yet again to life's
      turns-
      in the presence of this new
    company, I find yearnings
      anew- but
        alas the same as before
        here it goes !

Titties Unveiled

oh the great mystique
that lives within the mind
as one observes these relics
as pious aw I may not seem
I am a true devotee to this
divine creation
a life-giving splendor that
paints the castle walls milk-white
sweeps the nation both in televised
distribution and in private showing
These are those felt and those observed
mounting the chests of those
waving them freely in the beach
and those sweeping them under
cover in cubicle and in parade
musical
as a believe in love first and
foremost , it's only second nature
that titties go hand and hand

Sp aced-d

I dont know when it happened really.
 for the first time
 Maybe after having heard The Bangles
    but probably the first time I heard
    Pink Floyd
    that it'd really occurred to me
       where we were living
 This spacious tundra
    resting simultaneously on the tip of
  Davinci's finger
 & underneath Elvis' toupee

I'd declared myself maitred
      and you The man who'd fallen to earth
in every right as much David Bowie
      as you were Cher

  we'd wandered a little delirious thenceforth
       speaking broken spanish
     dipping toes in tide-pools
and wondering about the real dimensions
   of sinking sand pits and walden's pond
   we'd been just as much floating
   as we were sinking
    treading twinkling stars
    and Gallon hats

*"It was a gift for my boyfriend who I am still with. He has the
poem displayed with some other art and memorabilia next
to his computer where it gets read and appreciated daily. I
always loved Erika's use of imagery in this poem, beautiful
language and rhythm that conveys such a unique perspective.
In the brief moment Erika's path crossed mine, she was a kind
soul who spread love, beauty and art to two total strangers,
and I have no doubt she touched many others as well."*

I was piecing it together
 like a recipe
the slow churning manner of a
   crock pot

 nobody was feeding my
      open hearts
 blank slate with chalkboard
words, fresh like basil
I thought I'd known better than
 this, making a covenant
         with fictive motives
  until at last I'd surrendered
and made a pact
         and you appeared

Bukake Chess

This is a home invasion
a presentation of the fetishes
   so long left unexplored
   I've processed the possible
      outcomes, -
      pregnancies - ostrich egg sized growth
   a more sculpted form of handiwork
   as my teacup sized muscles grow
      just like the groin
   I'd gone against the grain
      some timeago, but its been years
      since I'd seen those whelping tears
      hugging cheekbones and eyelids alike
I must warn you of the disgruntled
   aftereffect laying in heaving
      hurt hangover from
   such an atomic event

Proud

we watch from a perch
intrigued and amused
bewildered by certain choices
but with the full understanding that only eternity can provide

You know now you can confide
in these heavens above
that the tides rise to greet you - when you think disaster is
coming,
you can roll downhill,
and just know
something
will catch you
that saving grace is more than a gesture

moving in

from a compilation of lush greens
a composition of
rural scene and scraping
metallic angles
I've found myself in this place
abounding in grace
and laughing faces
the landscape shift is so surreal
I find the structure in which to feel

"Our paths only crossed for a small moment in the grand scheme of life and yet, she had such an impact on myself and my boyfriend. We were new to the Austin area and decided to visit South Congress when we came across Erika giving out poems on a donation basis - I felt drawn to Erika and could not pass on the opportunity.

Our poems -- 'Proud' and 'moving in' -- are now framed in our little Austin apartment, they were the very first decoration we hung up on our blank walls. Erika truly inspired us as I'm sure she did many people"

where the stars have been
  absorbed backwards

it seems the night has been sheltered
  by man
  we've made painstaking attempts
perhaps not consciously
  at shielding ourselves from
    the glow of
      life
disturbed by its realness perhaps
    the way the circles are
    complete
      that nothing ever seems to
        die,
      try as hard as we may
we will never succeed

The Unconscious Mind

    Forgive me
when or if my affectation seems contrived
    my countenance on the flimsy-er side
for this
iceberg knows no end
    Clap for me
      when I attempt , mockingly
      to grasp for straws
      in a world full of
        overflowing fluids
    When I start belly-dancing
      at your mothers funeral
or joke about being two-faced then
        wake up with a sunburn on one side
    Forgive me
    father for my phantoms have
      grown operatic
my myrtles moaning
        and
    my dreams ever the more clever
  I've slipped on far too many
freudian bananas
    My fellowship knows no rings
but even then my heartstrings are
      singing

I said a special prayer
asking for home to appear
and there it was a household
  inexplicable
  in many ways
greatness
  embraced in each cushion
  welcomes me in
  back to Austin
    I click heels together
    and the fate is sealed

Only the Lonesome

I'd known something was missing
there seemed to be a gaping tear
    in the fabric of existence, or
    candy wrapper rather
    so I peered within seeing it
    was a necessary passageway
    a portal even with which
    life could be drawn within

I breathed in deeply for in Latin
'Spiritus' means breath
    & so finally I found the
    loneliness and left

Chillin'

time is of the essence
the time is now
together we can cross bounds
together we know no bounds
how beautiful
you are
its beyond romance
the intrigue raised
is from everyone
wondering how our love
can be so preserved
it pulls us back and forth to
and fro
we are riled into
a new space
the positive space is filled=

a Tequila Sunrise

morning greets us
but we'd not really slept yet
  we'd committed ourselves to
      a wild but all the while refined
        sort of experience
  Not drinking directly from the
      bottle,
  not sleeping it off on some strange
couch
  I've seen my makers mark
    in the seas of chance
      carried away into
        a unique romance
with a purer influence
          sort of

"Her poem ended up perfectly describing drinking and
romance and I felt it was a recollection of many nights I've
had. I keep this poem next to my bar area in my condo, so
each time I'm making cocktails or having drinks I end up
reading it."

A Concentrated Error

sometimes I feel the carriage
   of time
breaking down for a movement
  the once-fast-paced transportation
   method stalls out
the lumbering gait of the jolly
green man is terminated
     as he takes a midday nap
taking up somehow the entire
  freeway causing delays
worthy of broadcast
     He and I now become
friends
  after such a long butting of
heads , we've agreed that
     a change of pace is
  only for the best

Alien Curtsy

I'm a pretty rational
regular guy I'd say for the
most part
not endeared towards the
strange for the sake of it
nor towards meandering down
paths dark and uneven
but on occasion something
stumps the consenting
part of the mind
urges you towards belief
in the divine
A blue and glowy being
feral as a streetrat
as mystical as a gang
of octopi
Like I've said, I'm
just a decent guy- not
to negate what's plainly
exposed
I must share this
as clear as a whistle
blows

Use the Force

I'm going to take it to another
  level
    This time
  will be the first time i've used
    the force
    I've watched these things
     in play innumerable times
    the way the cosmos stir up
      genius
 I've lived wrong for so long
 not to employ this
    in the fashion bestowed by the
    Almighty
 love in its full-fledged form

"She truly showed us her talents and inspired me to draw/sketch photos inspired by her poem one day. I remember telling her that I would post art inspired by her poem and tag her on Instagram. She was really nice and kind."

I was lying to the moon
now I lie beneath it
  The Saharan dust feels like
    the moon's grit has descended
  in a desultory toss
    landing here
  forming the plains
    criss-crossed with brush
    and causeways
    calypsoing
I've left home , feeling almost
  as if something guided me to
 this resting place
The velvet ropes were barely
able to hold anyone
  inside
    even if it has been steel
  cables I'd've departed just
    the same

"We only spoke for a few moments, as she was busy typing away—but she was a beautiful soul and poet. I hope your family finds solace in her words, and I am certain she touched the hearts of many. This one she wrote for me gave me goosebumps"

Friends Delight

Another day spent in this ethereal place
  there is a special
   encore each time
    you spout that mess of language
    Its pacifying really
 to hear natures outbursts formulated
   in such sharp tongued quips
 Your acerbic negligence is charming
  really
  refreshing
   in a reality full of
  abstract and nonchalant parroting
   this is what makes the world
   continue
  honesty
    uncontained

Long Haul

long stretches of dawn and day
 spill out between us
   like milk mixed with engine oil
The little airports &
     turnstiles form intricate patterns
   over infinite fields
    Kids batter up
    and leave hours later with eyes
like discharged vets
      This is our land
  We stretch phone cords across it
   between one another
       playing house, playing cat and more
          being lovers
    The world is waking where you are
      as I am only now going to sleep

Cowboy Smile

There's something about the
    face of a real cowboy
  it projects visture's hardness
  It drives away the monsters
The cowboy is a stallion-
    a marksmen, a hitchhiker &
    a driver
    He is the face of the northern
    winds blowing
    The cottony dry refuges
    in the midst of long highways
      He is the face of all the
      other cowboys
      confidence in the storm

first love's embrace

where there was once passion,
    there still is
it does not simply disappear
    the sanctity imagined
from that initial repose
    the silent close of palm around flat
  open-faced
vulnerability around a sore-spot

this is how it goes
    before the rhythm has yet picked up
      before the long repertoire of loves
  has led to the steadiness of
    fearlessness

the first one is so fragile
    but just watch now as the layers
    build like rings in a tree stump

    and the surface of loves to come
  will be met by those
marbleized swirls

I'd traveled many a mile
to grow so content within
one day I'd realized
how much the traveling
engaged such an internal sentiment
from the North Carolina lines
to texan line dancers
from the swinging rhythms of
holes in the walls
to the nights spent like
lifetime long romances
we saw once upon a times
turn into sweet goodnights
but still I roam
never though, do I fully
say Goodbye

"She definitely had a gift for poetry, I was amazed at how she was able to write such an incredible poem in just a few minutes with her typewriter."

Teenage Love

cyber snapshots turned
eventually to
   the heartfelt conversations
that are shared only
   within the spaces between
   persons in the physical

      The
   attraction sincere
      has transformed into
      an even deeper endearment
      The excitement of love
      in these early years
        is a rush unmet by
        most activities

I chased them off
the red and blue colored wookies
   of the mind
  looking like EDM ragers
   as entertaining as an early 2000s
 screensaver or a
      fairly unique poinsettia
They scattered and now the door
   is open
  a light shines through and I emerge
        triumphant on a scene of
     fans I'd never then imagined
would be roaming these courtyards
       the other who'd fought
    the red and blue
  michelin man

*"It was the "first day" of a new chapter of my life—I was
on the tail end of one of those years that held so much
pain that at some points it felt unsurvivable. When I
approached Erika and asked her how it worked she
told me to just share a few words with her about what
was going on with me. I said something along the lines
of I was at the beginning of a new beginning, and I had
fought really hard to get there. She got to writing on her
typewriter. When she handed me the poem, it was like
she had gone into my head and put words to everything
I had been through lately. I cried when I read it. Erika
was lovely and warm and sweet and kind and talented,
above all. Her poem now lives on my fridge; it was the
first thing that I stuck up. Next to it now are Polaroids
and stickers and other things that make me smile."*

The Sun's Glow

welcome to the black parade
a world apart from ours where no life
  lives
  the rain reigns, thunderous trains
of furious lightning criss cross like
  electrical wires bleaching a
  midnight sky
I like the next day
    the sun, coy as a nymph
shows its eager face
  much like that of a child
      floods the atmosphere
        with an urgency much more
      swiftly than rain

Fred-ly

He is more than friendly
He is Fred-ly
a free energy source for all that
encounter him
illuminating
with just a glimpse into his eyes
sparkling and liberated
A breath of fresh air for
     those caught up on the limited
tied down by nothing except for
     the occasional whim
He's a reminder , a bridge between
  the physical realm and the eternal

Otter Odyssey

we embark on a magical mystery
            tour
with otters on the mind
these little angel sprites
  live in worlds of rivers
careening through with ease
  holding onto their rocks
    each chosen as personal tokens
      They wrap tiny paws around
      clams
  and engage in otter love affair
      not too far apart
  from we 'civilized' beings
we may even consider them
  friends
learning more and more about
  how to live well
      with them as examples of
      excellence

*"This poem is so very special to me and my boyfriend, we
always say how no one knows but me, him & Erika. And
how amazingly talented you have to be to write something so
special within minutes. we would like everyone to know this
poem, so people can get a glimpse of how special & talented
she was and how she impacted peoples lives even if it was just
a couple of minutes exchanging words and leaving us with a
poem we will cherish forever."*

Birthday on the rise

we coast along this precipice in time
Together
merciful to our pasts
not yet
reproachful towards our future misgivings
not
yet certain of them either
It seems the more we realize
that our mistakes are unavoidable
they become less jarring
we forgive and through the intercession
of our ease
and that of the universe's eternal love
we make less mistakes as a result

Met You in the Middle

It wasn't the dawn of my life
nor midday even-
more about noontime, when you'd
appeared
attending to my branches
wearing britches and digging trenches
for a furtherance of hydration
Sensational, you were in tune instantly
with the act of creation
Drawing from within me,
a new sense of liveliness
finding the best aspects and
sharpening their edges
forgiving the wrinkles
from the past's discontinuities

Reeling it in

who would've thought
such simplicity would take away
complexities bermuda triangles
remedying pains beyond measure
far overdue and past occupying oneself
with
the dog with its 2 year old brain
and outstanding level of adoration
brings life to life
reorients us with the sweetness
that always is present
hardly is it that we presume
the love they exude was
always in the room

Freedom soars on birds wings

it doesn't dwell in the soot
  the ancient world comes
 trickling up through
    the mud nonetheless
 giving all a fair change
    for change to
    grip onto
  first a penny finds my fingers
then a dollar
 then I'm wandering again like
    davy crockett
      though I don't have much
   I am all of it.

Exceeding Expectations

this worlds been breeding
 a vast assortment of ideas
 and its expecting
 drinking a fine diet of brandy
   speaking of the outsourced passions
     of an abrasive tongue
speckled with cordiality's impositions
      bracing itself as the
whirlwinds pick up on rollercoaster
slides
I hope for heaven
though it's not far
   I find myself draped in
    weathered raiment after millenia
   of reincarnation
     and hell's hurdles fling wayward
         with the wind
as soon as I see heaven within

Changes on the Rise

    I know it's true
as few concepts may be
that what you give, you may receive
    in return
  (at least in some form)

    I'd grown as it were,
   married to this sport
   dedicating both time and efforts
   expensive
   but time has shown
     revealed unto me plainly
that it will pay
 off
   as surely as the years are long

"Erika seemed to be an incredible human from the momentary interaction we had."

Making a Racket

I heard a sound amongst the
regular dreary ambient noises
  of backyard midnight
someone creeping
perhaps in your typical burglar
    get-up
a vocalization on much like a
  caricature of a snarl
a wasted wretch
  much like myself perhaps
stalking the basil plants
    organizing trash
it turned out my investigational
    skills wereNt as sharp as once
    I'd (atleast) perceived them to
be
    this was no goat-eed stranger
    this was a racoon family

Taking on the Big Town

now it was big time
we were making time
and the days were bright and blue and
bleary
no room for tears
but it was as if our visions
had been airbrushed
photoshopped for optimal brightness
and contriteness
I'd seen the
times change
the city itself turn to a maze

GoLightly

step with the
  grace bestowed to you
    now walk faster
    now don't listen to these requests
    They are from some arbitrary
      wielder of power
there is only one true holder
    of all things
and now so generously he extends
a hand
  fingers like light beams
      offering you everything

"I had recently moved to a little apartment off South Congress. I was walking through the streets not really noticing anything until I walked pasted Erika ... right outside of Güeros. With a big smile she said "hiiii". I cannot describe to you how warm that hi felt. I instantly felt connected to her and seen in that moment. I didn't even notice her typewriter at first, thinking she was an artist making jewelry or paintings like usual on Soco or just a random stranger. She said, "I write poems. You pick a topic and I write about it."

I felt a lightness in her presence, so I gave that as my topic. When I read her poem, it was so profound, almost a kind of therapy.

Erika is proof that there is some strange magic behind seemingly coincidental encounters."

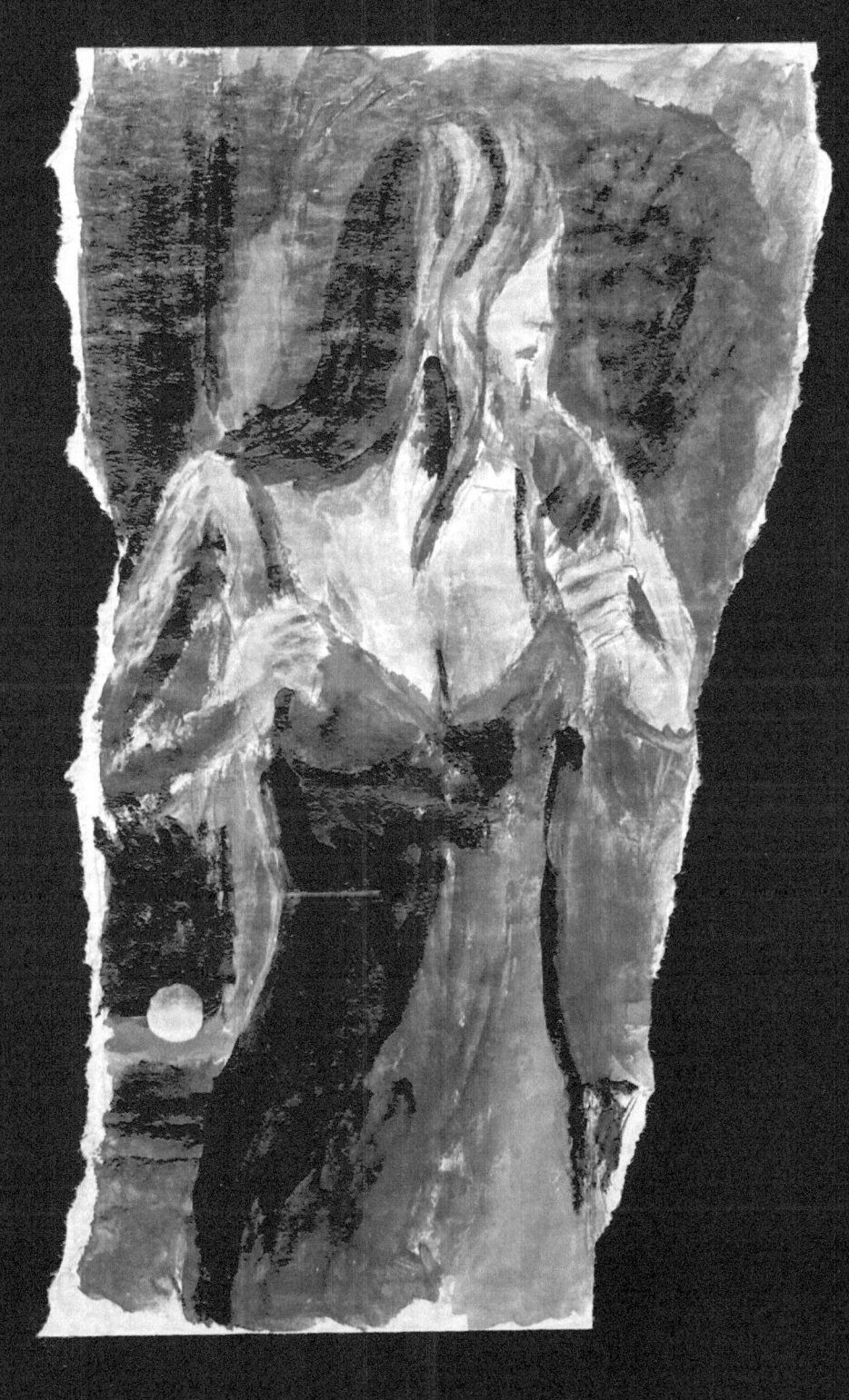

friends- not so distant

though the paths have been
rocky in our pasts
at last
at long last, we've made it
through tribulations
swatting at the corruptible
seedlings as they dropped
intents of implanting
anything other than our
dreams
and now here goes
what we've made of it
Taking the reels of
education, pinning
them to our hearts and
using them as payment
for rent in a space
that we'd once only
dreamed of- though we may be
physically away, we can share
now instead- two separate
spaces

"It's something I'll always treasure."

From the Beach to Route 66
from dessert spanning
  to no need for planning
 we keep it moving in the spirit
  but do not let the simplicity deceive
   This comes from years of wisdom
     compiled
    an ascendency we could not avoid
     neglecting the 'void'
    knowing , instead
  fulness

Falling in Love

What's lost in Translation
is soon overcome
from the barrel of the gun
    misfiring to the target
I at times accidentally annihilate
the light with a shadow
of residual
a conflict of interests
    Stoic as I may be
when it comes down to
performance
    this is no act
        this is my heart bare
hanging by threads
    stronger than life itself
    love is the only thing
    that keeps the
        whites of my eyes visible
the wisdom to try
        where cynicism ties
        can no longer lie

What's in Store

well, we know what's already
  happened- what sits resting
  in the cubby-holes of our
  imaginations rest-stops
those places we visit in passing
  after night's fallen
  & yawns commend sleep's embrace
  we know where we've gone
separately, but mostly we know
  where we've gone together
      the mind's imprints doubled
    from the addition of another to
    the timeline
  & so we've seen those lines
  etching maps into our minds
  but know we walk those cosways
    and press on

Crafted

from thin air
but my wallet and life grew all the
more thicker
the filming zeroes in
the crowd grows in wild wonder
tuning in from beginning to end
just a quick few seconds
but the message is clear
the rattle of bones in the pot
the searing of tunaskin
the only thing they miss is
the smell
hanging in the air

A Grip of Gray

What was once subdued, a heap of
depression invoking gray matter
now it seems to me, middle-ground
less so poverty
and more like a limbo
the straggle of streetwalkers
the long arms with knuckles dragging against
the gray of pavement
the sky is streaked with flares of
sun, a paling reminder of
what was once daytime
and now I see,
I cannot just wait here absent-mindedly
for the sun to come
to be freed.

Ready to Roll

here it is
the long awaited
  and yet suddenly accessible
    the 'too good to be trues'
  and uplifted sprees of polyphony
  resound in robust whorls
  it turns out
    the truth is more solid than those
fictions of before
      those scary and weirds only
        corrupt byproducts of childhood
            fictions
            these love-filled realms
            are less obscene
              and larger than those 8-bit
            characters
          layers are shed
          life is met

Life returning

happiness always had existed in happenstance
   round the parameters
 and like a dream reappointed
   the veil had been lifted

    I'd
 seen you sountering as a pearl
 now turning an opalescent churn

   charms once so
     much like chandeliers
   become as clear as daylight

 excuse me
 and welcome to the show
   it had shuffled in as eagerly
   as closing time has shuffled us out
   eschewing ourselves from barred windows
   into a park
   reset into direction

The Moon

  its many faces
shift not only the oceanic plains
    stirring up coral like tumbleweed
     blowing in the wind
     but also it changes the mind's tides
    on a global scale
     the lunatics
      holler through
      the thick blankets of
       evening
    but peace is easily
     restored
    as soon as morning turns

Tumbled and torn

Deep in the brawn
the tenuous ripples of
  lawn meets evergreen
  the areas subterranean
under a canopy of endless night
  bespeckled with star after star
after metermaid and meteor alike

  draped with a pilt oil
and token shards of granite
    the tumbleweeds
      are spin-dried
  in the fluid embrace
  or the red hot sun

He goes off

sojourning into waters uncharted
   a staff in his hand
   like some mythologized
  sentinel

He brings good tidings on his
    journeys
strikingly handsome
  but alas even further
making even the simple not
   of identifying a leaf
    a work of art
   saying F*k this week,
   allthewhile
   redefining it

What's Not for Show

Though wehave an unbridaled
sense of how to create
romantic vacation photos
Capturing the sublime
and reducing it to pixels,
we short
and silly folk
have more that goes on
just under the nose
It(s not that its intentionally
left under the radar
it's just that simply we
are so small in stature
but even then
our love is louder
than any filter

Caught in the mold

we'd traversed the deepest pits of
  this countryside
ramming our heads along from taboo tavern
to trundlebed
from seeing terrors
familiar to readers of ripleys believe
    it - or Not
but the greatest lives in that indistinct
and glossy film
maquillaged onto the ripe peachy colored
sternums of hotel Jackfruits
and pink ladies
and upon the tinted windows
  and glasses alike
of those lost in indiscriminate
revery and introspection
caught on the verge of
a fence soon
to fall

"Erika was a beautiful soul. I keep the poem framed next to my bed. May she live forever in the words that she wrote <3"

Rallied up

mark your tallies down
the sounds of our galloping
arrested by nothing
except the occasional glint of past
embellishments
We are like texas cowboys
quicker than the law
's) of gravity
Our prized
nobility thrown asunder
rivals not the promise fo freedom
here the road
cantankerous
and woosome
takes and absorbs all

All in the Family

it's in the eyes
 where sincerity's rush ushers in
     a special surrender
     our big silly family
     loves this guy
with his 'embarrassing' antics
     in public spaces
       we've speculated on those that
       came before
     concerns raised have gone out the
     window
  he lays it all out
        an open book

Bella Babe

at the sound of 'popsicle'
 her eyes ignite
   with the delicate
   sort of excitement that
   babies best embody

 She loves to ride her bicycle
something surprising to
    have on the resume of
    a being so young
    and so dear
she cherishes sweet Patrick
   she holds him closely
 as both of them share the
   fact that they are friend
to both the contented and the
      lonely

copy by Erika Evans of original painting by Martina Shapiro;
used with permission of Martina Shapiro

SOLO POEMS

Erika's family found these poems among her
things. They are all very likely poems that Erika
wrote on her own, rather than for someone
else. All were written on a typewriter; as with
the previous poems, the original formatting is
preserved as much as possible.

Anniversary Dawning

Here we are still
after so many impassioned
     conversations
building together as it were
  a configuration of love
     so divine, so precise
     mirrored to nature's whims
the I love you so
   much of
      calypso-ing graffiti
     that
       eager shuffle of feelings
   unveiled
draws us back into this shared
     space, uninhabited by
   any other

we'd surrendered sweetly

I've found myself with her
  in the eye of the hurricane
  This one here— with all the
  eloquence and refinement of royalty
  has a way about her
    that with just a smile
  she reminds me of everything
    decent, everything that is
    beautiful
She has such a calmness about her
that our surroundings just follow
  suit
  In our kingdom together
  harmony ensues
  and the only Law
  is that of Love

soaking in all the moon's lights
hanging low
　I feel the tides in my mind's eyes
　　drifting in the tumult
　but as the sun rises yet again
I find my efforts
　have not been remiss
all the
time in eternity
　and now I am bound within it
　written into its pages
underneath
the moon's phases

Weddings

it's an epidemic
  unparalleled are the numbers
    falling into the statistics
    even higher the rates of bachelorette
      parties than there are divorces
          these-a-days
  sweeping the nation
    like the swine flu had been
    rumored to
      I've considered it myself
    once or twice
  but to really truly be
committed
  get ready with all the faith
you can muster

ever deepening gaze

    The years have gone by
      and with each subsequent
      rotation
      I've found another ring in your
      eye, like those in lumber
  I've been witnessing your wisening
      been christened by
the way we speak
      there is something holy here
       between us
      divinity has made its mark

Crisis in Action

This is not an act of Love
    this is passion unextinguishable
    an overactive ego driven by
    heartless ambition
I have a positive space seat
    on a flight to Fresno
    but I keep checking the
memos – Your eyes ignite each time
    I look at the phone
  stirring up chaos unchained
    You like to maim the moment
      rid the air of its lightness
    crushing the stars
    feeding them Xanax
      hurling
    pancake batter
  at the love I had imagined for us

Spacious

I wanted to venture to Saturn's
Edges, but y'know it's not
  so simple
 at least in the physical
  body

   someone mentioned lucid
    spells of dream escapades
 a zealous character maybe
But I took him up on the offer
   with a hand extended
 soon we were in full stride
   slapping the constellations
with hooves of gold

Dad

He was quite the lad
  still extent in many
  folks' memories
  He is strong in faith
    wise,
  teaching those who'd
  encountered him about
 greater things
He carried this with him
a walking encyclopedia
    in a sense
  thrifting those unusual
artifacts
 making sense of life
  where others were unsure
He had words reassuring
 brought peace and
  understanding
    those things more
   precious than gold

i see

Those things from before
that I was blind to
they've become redefined
    and the light is shed upon
  those who think themselves wise
Those who came before
    into my vicinity
I'd had an affinity before towards
    them but now it's discernment
I'd lost from myself that
  widowy peak of careless
      over concentration
and found instead
      with all of this
      a peace of mind

A dream (no more than that)

You're more than a mother
  more than a CEO
    And what was of chief importance
    you'd said as you gathered no moss
    was to live life like the quest
      it is
    dealing so impressively well with
    the remnants of plight
    setting them aside
      integrating a modest cynicism
        into your wise heart
  without forgoing such a vibrant
    spirit
    you're more than the dream
    You are the dreamer,
  the believer,
    and the sophisticated one.

Her name is Joanna
a straight shooter
    she doesn't spare words of
        wisdom
They come flowing out of her
with the sort of ease that only
    comes from those with
    deep familial love
We'd seen
    the 2010 World Series game
        together
 and as it was beginning
 I knew this memory would last
etched forever into my mind
  as if divinity had scrawled it

Spawned from What?

where do these ideas come from
  emerging as if from thin air
sometimes I wonder,
  who really is their creator
The narrative arc so complex
  seems to have been developed
by some savant script writer
maybe he's a
  giant, maybe a shrimp
either way, his ways
  are unkempt

The road we travel

I didn't know what we were getting into
    not til I heard that faint
  mischievous laugh of yours
    it seemed something greater on
     the horizon awaited
      and the worlds we'd seen apart
    have now converged
     the flash of things
      brassy and bold
  is now consoled
    and our hearts grow younger
    than before

That lavish life I'd seen before
now meets me underneath this roof
a certain sort of structure has
    formed tying knots with
        ancestral lines

The beams are made of hearty wood
    the foundation is fine cement
        the windows overlook a vista
of all that is to come
        with you
    I have some foresight
        with you, I find my home

Number 1

she and I,
we seem to go way back
it's as if we've known each other
  from many years ago
    We both execute decisions with
      logic, not impulse
    though it may be as black and white
    as a Rohrschach
      we still find the urge to laugh
    in our connection there's
a Venn-Diagrammatic structure
  where peace is king
    and all the rest is second
        in command.

Frijoles and Cheese

it's simple really
though carbs may be considered
complex
the taco's contents love their life
in their little home— the shell
I once had
been
amazed at concoctions very strange
but whatever reason
lately I've been drawn back to
the beans and cheese and
tortillas
for better days

Communicable Ease

I've at times questioned these
  lines scattered,
    sitting adjacent to the
      broken glass of events
      turned to theatrics
I've wondered at the
ways we've wandered but
  You and I,
  regardless of the changing tides
  have
  found an island to sit atop
gazing at the sea

Traveling through Spaces

I live in a universe duplicitous
   as it is expansive
   & so in order to confront that
    I venture into the crannies and
   nooks of cluttered portals
Going where others deem unconventional
     or outright mad

bird watching
(if you will)

About the Author

(written by Erika for her 2021 book *Eat Like a Local: Austin*)

Erika is a traveler, writer, musician, and visual artist. Born in Austin in '96, she moved to Louisiana at the age of 11, then back to Austin for the full-blown UT Austin college experience. She's resided on and off the last 6 years there working as an artist.

Erika enjoys birdwatchin', hitchhikin', electric scooterin' uphill wearing a man's leather jacket with pockets full of beers, and skydiving. She enjoys the literature of Joyce. She's a newfound bible enthusiast and Erik Andre Show lover, an unlikely combo. She likes to stretch the sinews of the 'known' world.

Having retired briefly from a year-long series of exploits around the US, she writes to keep the dream alive.

acknowledgements

This book would not have been possible without:

Erika's sister Kate, who reached out to many of Erika's poem recipients and transcribed the poems from their original form for this book.

Photographer Antonio Jimenez, for his wonderful short video of Erika titled "the poet."

"the poet"

Olivia Hammerman and her generous donation of designing the book's cover. See more of her work at www.ochbookdesign.com

And finally, all the people who stopped by Erika's poetry table to get a poem.

Burlwood Books is a small independent press in Austin, Texas. We are dedicated to art that celebrates the messy, vibrant, mistake-filled wonder of life.